The 7 Day

Brain Booster

J. Alexander

*Hodder
Children's
Books*

A division of Hachette Children's Books

First published in Great Britain in 2007 by Hodder Children's Books

This edition published by Hodder Children's Books in 2007

Text copyright © Jenny Alexander 2007
Illustration copyright © David Whittle 2007
Design by Don Martin

The rights of Jenny Alexander and David Whittle to be identified as
the Author and Illustrator of this Work have been asserted by them
in accordance with the Copyright, Designs and Patents Act 1988.

4

A catalogue record for this book is available from the British Library.

ISBN-13: 978 0 340 93069 4

Printed and bound by CPI Bookmarque Ltd, Croydon, Surrey

The paper and board used in this paperback by Hodder Children's Books are
natural recyclable products made from wood grown in sustainable forests. The
manufacturing processes conform to the environmental regulations of the
country of origin.

Hodder Children's Books
A division of Hachette Children's Books
338 Euston Road, London NW1 3BH
An Hachette UK Company
www.hachette.co.uk

CONTENTS

Other titles in the Seven Day series:

The Seven Day Self Esteem Super-Booster
The Seven Day Bully-Buster
The Seven Day Stress Buster

INTRODUCTION

About brain boosting

Since you've picked up this book I'm guessing you want to be a whiz at schoolwork. Or maybe your mum and dad bought the book for you, or your teacher put it in the class library, because they want you to be a whiz as well.

Everyone wants you to do well because then you'll pass lots of exams and be able to do whatever you want when you grow up.

The normal way of trying to get kids to do better at school is by piling on the homework, buying revision guides and getting extra tuition. Does that thought fill you with enthusiasm?

Of course not! And it doesn't fire your brain up either. In fact, it's enough to make your brain go out on strike! Schoolwork is important – but you already get plenty of it at school.

If you go crashing on with too much schoolwork at home

- you have less time to do other important things

- you miss out on social time with your family and friends

- you and your parents can get into a stress

- it can actually put you off learning

Too much swotting can make your brain go stodgy, like Daniel's Christmas cake ...

Daniel's Christmas cake

Every year, Daniel helped his mum to make the Christmas cake, until finally he got old enough to do it on his own. 'This is going to be the best Christmas cake ever,' he thought.

He weighed out the ingredients carefully until he came to the black treacle. Not everyone likes black treacle, but Daniel loved it, so he reckoned the more he put in the better the cake would be. Instead of one spoonful like the recipe said, he put in the whole tin! The cake came out of the oven looking and smelling great.

But then it's Christmas. 'Who'd like some cake?' asks Daniel. His mum gets the sharp knife. She tries to stick it in ... She pushes hard ... She stands up and puts her weight behind it. The cake is as hard as a brick.

INTRODUCTION

The moral of the story? **More isn't always better.**

'So what am I supposed to do, then?' I hear you say. 'I want to get great grades!' The answer is

- trust your teacher to give you all the practice you need to cover the curriculum and do well in tests

- don't bash your brains with extra study and revision at home

- pump up your brain-power generally so stuff like tests and new subjects feel much easier

This is the art of brain-boosting!

The art of brain-boosting

You only spend about 15% of your time at school but your brain is learning all the time ... because it wants to! Your brain is by nature an intrepid explorer, constantly investigating unfamiliar territory and coming back with new information and knowledge. You don't know what your new mobile can do? Your brain wants to find out! You don't know what's on TV tonight? Your brain wants to find out!

If you want to have a happy, healthy brain, you have to give it the freedom to do what comes naturally instead of forcing it to keep going over the same ground, and help it build up the seven super strengths a truly top explorer needs.

The seven super strengths:

1. Self-belief

2. Courage to face the unknown

3. A good memory

4. A healthy body

5. Knowing when to take a break

6. Having a team

7. Having a dream

There are seven super strengths and by a happy coincidence there are also seven days in a week – which brings me to the beauty of this book ...

About this book

The Brain-booster has seven chapters – one for each day of the week – and each chapter covers one of the qualities your brain needs to achieve its full learning potential. All you have to do is read a chapter a day and pick an activity from the list at the end.

It's as easy as ABC –

A Before you go to bed, read the chapter for the following day and decide which activity you're going to do.

B When you get up in the morning, remind yourself what it is.

C Some time during the day, do it!

Note: It's best to start on a Sunday evening, so if you're reading this on a Wednesday, sorry – you're just going to have to wait!

The 'seven day' system

'Wow!' I hear you say. 'This means I can pump up my brain power in just one week!' Well, no ... Brain-boosting is about practice, not theory, and the more you do it the better you get. So when you get to Sunday, you start all over again, choosing different activities.

By the end of the second week, you won't have to reread the chapters any more because they're very short and you'll be able to remember what's in them. You can just choose your exploration for each day and do it.

There are enough activities for a different one every day for ten weeks. If that sounds like a bit of a mission, don't worry – they're all v. quick and simple, designed to help you build up your brain-power like Amundsen pushing for the South Pole, one step at a time.

Two top brain-boosting tips

1   Try to have a go at as many different activities as you can, but skip any that really don't appeal to you – enjoyment is the key to success.

2   Try not to miss a day. It's much better to do a really quick activity you've done before than nothing at all.

One week will make a difference, two weeks will make twice the difference – the longer you keep it up the more confident and competent you'll feel.

Ten treats for ten weeks

If you decide to try for the full ten weeks give yourself a little incentive. Every Sunday, buy a small treat and wrap it up like a present. Put it somewhere safe.

If you're doing the brain-booster with a mate, buy a little gift for each other or if you've got the sort of mum/dad/grandma/grandpa/friend who likes helping, ask them to do it for you.

At the end of ten weeks brain-boosting it'll be like Christmas – you'll have ten lovely treats to unwrap and enjoy!

The seven-day system is brilliant because:

- **It's easy**

    The activities take only a few minutes each day.

- **It works**

    It's not about swotting up for tests and trying to convince people you're clever – it's about getting your brain in tip-top condition and really being clever, so that learning is easier and you have to do hardly any swotting up at all.

- **It gives you skills for life**

    The art of brain-boosting isn't just about getting a handle on schoolwork – it bumps up your learning skills for life.

The seven-day brain-boosting club

The seven-day approach is very flexible. You can do it by yourself if you like doing things on your own, but it's also great to share with other people.

You can do the brain-booster with your best mate or a group of friends, and compare notes afterwards. You can do it with your mum or dad if you're in a family that likes doing things together. You can ask your teacher to set up a seven-day brain-boosting club at school.

It doesn't matter how you do it, as soon as you start you'll be part of the global seven day brain-boosting club because everyone who's got this book, wherever they are in the world, will be choosing from the same choice of activities on the same day as you. Imagine!

Ready, steady ... reminder time

Unless you happen to be reading this on a Sunday evening, it's time to close the book now. Leave yourself a reminder to start on Sunday somewhere you can't miss it – on your mobile, say, or a note beside the bed.

Ttfn! *

*Ta ta for now

INTRODUCTION

I said, close the book! Still, I knew you wouldn't, so here are some things you could do in the meantime while you're waiting to get started on Sunday.

1 Get a special note pad

You can use this like an explorer's log, to record your progress and observations as well as doing any writing or drawing tasks.
You might want to keep it private, like a diary so ...

2 Find a secret hiding place

For your notepad, not for you! Don't be slack and just shove it in your undies drawer – that's so unimaginative and besides, your mum will find it the next time she tries to match up all the odd socks.

3 Make a record sheet

This is just for people who either like keeping
record sheets or won't be able to remember
which activities they've done without one.

You could do it at the back of your special
note pad if you've got one.

	Mon	Tues	Wed	Thurs	Fri	Sat	Sun
Week 1	5	2	10	4	2	7	6
2							
3							
4							
5							
6							
7							
8							
9							
10							

4 Think about getting some brain-booster buddies

If you decide someone you know might want
to join in, get them on board now before you
begin.

I think that just about does it, so now you really
must close the book until Sunday evening, OK? I
mean it!

1 MONDAY

Get in the zone

Here's something you don't often have a chance to do – write your own school report! Think about it carefully and give yourself marks out of five.

1 = absolutely awful
2 = poor
3 = average
4 = pretty good
5 = brilliant

SCHOOL REPORT

NAME .... *Me!*

SUBJECT .... *Schoolwork*

1 UNDERSTANDING ..../5

2 EFFORT ..../5

3 KEENNESS ..../5

4 CONFIDENCE ..../5

5 ABILITY TO
   REMEMBER THINGS ..../5

TOTAL ..../25

If your *total score* was nearest to 5, you think you're generally awful at schoolwork; and if it was nearest to 10, you think you're poor. Nearest to 15, OK, you're average; nearest to 20, you're pretty good. If your score was almost 25 then you're really lucky – when it comes to schoolwork, you're 'in the zone'.

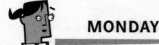

A person is 'in the zone' when they're doing something they find really interesting and absorbing. 'In the zone' *everyone* is a fantastic learner, but lots of people don't get that experience in all their school subjects.

How easily you learn something doesn't depend on how brainy you are but on how interesting you find it. Sometimes, you can get the idea that you're not very good at learning when actually the only problem is that you aren't very interested in

the subject. Then your confidence can take a knock, and things can go from bad to worse. If you think you're no good at learning you're likely to stop trying, and then you really won't be any good.

If you know you're a good learner you can weather the dull bits at school and throw yourself whole-heartedly into the things you enjoy. The best way to notice how good you are is by developing your hobbies and interests.

It doesn't matter what your passion is – football, horses, reading, celeb-watching, or just having a good gossip ...

... your ability to recall random facts about things you're interested in is astonishing!

Hobbies and interests

You might think you haven't got any interests and hobbies but if so, think again! Do you follow a TV soap or series? Do you like playing computer games? Do you keep a pet, read adventure stories, follow fashion, listen to music, have a family pastime like hill-walking or badminton? Everyone is interested in something.

Once you start becoming more aware of what things fire you up, you may be surprised to realise how much you know about them. If you're a Neighbours fan, for example, I bet you know all about what's going on in Ramsay Street, the characters, the layout of the houses, the latest feuds and funny plot-lines. If you're a horse-rider you'll know all sorts of things about looking after horses, racing, dressage, point-to-point – stuff that most people wouldn't have the first idea about. If you're keen on footie you might even understand the offside rule!

Think of something you're interested in at the moment. Now write your own 'hobby report'.

HOBBY REPORT

NAME .... *Me!* ....

SUBJECT ....
for example: guides/scouts, The Simpsons,
your best computer game

1	UNDERSTANDING	....../5
2	EFFORT	....../5
3	KEENNESS	....../5
4	CONFIDENCE	....../5
5	ABILITY TO REMEMBER THINGS	....../5

TOTAL ..../25

If you got a higher total score than
in your school report, I rest my
case! However good or bad you feel
you are at schoolwork, hobbies and
interests are the place where you are
most likely to experience yourself as
a fantabuloso learner.

Maybe you'll say, 'But that's just something I do – it isn't important.' Well, excuse me! It's all learning – and what's more it's the best possible kind of learning because –

1 It feels natural

You're free to follow your natural curiosity wherever it takes you and no further. Once you get bored, you drop that line of exploration and get into something different instead. For example, say you're fed up with the Tudors after a few days – that's too bad! You're stuck with them till you've covered the curriculum. But if you get fed up of finding out everything you can about your fave celeb at home you can forget about them and simply choose a different one to find out about.

2 It's easy

You build up your knowledge and skills quickly – and the more you know the easier it is to learn. That's because learning is like a jigsaw puzzle – every new piece fits in somewhere and the more you can see of the big picture, the easier it is to see where the piece should go.

3 It's exciting

With hobbies and interests, nobody tells you what to do. You're following your own leads and finding your own unique treasure trove of knowledge.

Hobbies give you the experience of being a great learner and that's good news for your schoolwork because it helps you feel more confident. Plus there's often also some icing on the cake.

The icing on the cake

Following your own interests can boost your school success because it often involves using all the literacy and numeracy skills you learn in school, without even noticing you're doing it. Great practice – and totally painless!

Take Ryan, for example. He doesn't see the point in most of his school subjects but look how many of them he uses in following his fave football club.

Ryan

Ryan eats, breathes and sleeps Leeds United. When he isn't on the club website or swapping football jokes with his mates online, he's flicking through his collection of programmes and fanzines or playing football trivia cards with his bro.

On his bedroom wall Ryan has a big map of the UK with all the premiership grounds marked on it; this year's fixtures list; signed photos and letters from players he's written to; and a graph of league positions so he can record how well Leeds are doing week by week compared with the same stage last season.

'If you think you can or you can't, you're right'

This is a quote from Henry Ford – head of the mega successful Ford Motor Company, and it's soooo true. If you want to be a great learner you've got to believe you can do it. If you don't think you can ... get some hobbies! Everyone can be brilliant when they're doing something that fires them up, and knowing you can be brilliant doing your own thing opens the way to being brilliant at school as well.

Get in the zone right now and boost your self-belief by choosing your Monday activity.

MONDAY ACTIVITIES

Choice of Monday activities

❶ Your special subject trivia quiz

Think of something you're interested in, like David Beckham for example, or cats, or cricket, or clothes. Test your knowledge.

Write down five questions about your special subject that you know the answers to and then write down the answers.

Give yourself a big 'Well done!' 5 out of 5 – you're a winner!

❷ 'I wonder ...'

Try to notice at least one time during the day when you think, 'I wonder ...' and follow through by finding out.

Say you come across the word 'irksome' in the book you're reading and you wonder what it means. Don't skip over it – get a dictionary and look it up (if you don't know what it means, that could be one of your 'I wonder ...'s)

Say your teacher's trying to explain something and you think, 'I wonder what she's talking about?' Ask!

Or your mate's got some tunes by a new band on his mp3 and you think, 'I wonder what they sound like?' Get him to give you a listen.

❸ Do a jigsaw!

Do a jigsaw and experience how learning works, building your knowledge 'picture' bit by bit, piecing things together, starting in a muddle and becoming easier as you go on.

Note: If you haven't got a jigsaw you can get one from the library or borrow one from a friend.

Another note: Let your mum / dad / sis / bro / mate join in if they want to – jigsaws can be fun to do with other people, just like learning.

❹ Plan a project

Write a list of all the ways you could develop your hobby or interest into a big project, like Ryan in this chapter. See how many lovely literacy and numeracy skills you could use – letters, stories, commentaries, graphs, tables, diagrams ...

Note: There's no need to stop at the planning stage – get stuck in if you like the idea of it!

❺ Find out where

Be on the look out today for an unfamiliar place – maybe the book you're reading is set in Paris, or your mate's on holiday in Devon, or the man on the News is talking about a famine in Chad.

Look online or in an atlas – follow your natural curiosity and find out exactly where it is.

❻ Root and branch

Write down all the things you can think of that you used to love doing but don't do any more. Then write down all the things you love doing now. Finally, list the things you'd like to try in the future.

Can you spot any common threads? Maybe you used to love painting and now your hobby's photography – they're both arty. Maybe you used to love swimming but now you play more tennis – they're both sporty.

Often your first hobbies and interests don't really disappear, they just develop, and eventually they may blossom into the work you choose to do when you grow up.

❼ Who, what, where, when, how and why?

Talk to a mate or family member about their fave pastime. Ask them six questions about it, starting with who, what, where, when, how and why. 'Who first got you into fly fishing? What does 'fly fishing' mean? Where do you mostly go to do it ...?'

❽ Could be interesting ...

Think of something you might be interested in but don't know much about, such as basketball or Iceland or keeping tortoises.

Write down all the ways you could find out more about it – for example, if you're interested in tortoises, do you know someone who's got one? If not, could you see if any of your family or friends know any tortoise-owners? Then there are books, websites, your local pet shop or animal park ...

Choose one way of finding out more and see what you can discover.

❾ 'I am a fantastic learner!'

Look at all the things you've learnt already, from basic skills like how to clean your teeth to complicated ones like how to read and write. You're amazing!

Make sure you don't forget that fact by telling yourself first thing in the morning and every time you think of it throughout the day, 'I am a fantastic learner!'

Note: If you think you might need a nudge, draw a dot on your thumbnail. Then every time you see it you'll remember what you have to do.

⑩ **Notice what you know**

Write down where you live and who lives in your house. Ask yourself, 'What special knowledge have I got, simply because of where I live and who I live with?' Jot down everything you can think of.

Say you live near the sea, you'll know about tides and boats and things you might find on a beach, whereas city-dwellers would know more about staying safe in traffic and where to shop.

Say you've got four younger brothers and sisters, you'll know all about babies and living in a big family. Or maybe your parents don't live together and you've got step-brothers and sisters, so you'll know about all that.

Say your mum's a traffic warden and your dad's a nurse – those are two jobs you'll know lots about. Or your big bro's a karate brown-belt, or your little sis does ballet ...

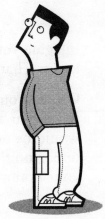

Note: Don't forget to include your pets.

2 TUESDAY

Embrace ignorance

Imagine you knew everything there was to know. That would be great, right? Wrong!

OK, so you wouldn't have to go to school, but if you already knew everything there would be no mysteries, no surprises and no opportunities to grow. You'd be bored out of your brains.

Luckily, no one can ever know everything – ignorance is a fact of life. And when it comes to brain-boosting, ignorance is bliss!

Ignorance is bliss

Ignorance is bliss because it means there's always something to discover, and that's exciting. The brainiest people aren't worried about not knowing things – they love it, because they see everything they don't know as an opportunity to learn something new.

31

Brain-boosters have to feel OK about not knowing things and see ignorance as a step on the road to knowledge. Check if you've got the right attitude by doing the 'not sure' quiz.

The 'not sure' quiz

Your teacher asks the whole class a question and you think you know the answer but you aren't sure. Do you

1 Act like you know it only you can't be bothered to put your hand up.

2 Wish she'd just get on with it and tell you.

3 Put your hand up – you might get it right.

4 Hide under the table.

Your mates are playing a new game and you're not sure how to play it. Do you

1   Pretend you know the game only you don't fancy joining in.

2   Try to get them to play a game you know instead.

3   Ask them to teach you.

4   Scuttle off, feeling stupid.

Your mum asks you to help her with a computer problem and you're not sure you'll know how to. Do you

1   Say anyone should know that, even her, and leave her to it.

2   Glance at the screen and give up.

3   Have a go – you might be able to fix it.

4   Get cross with her for asking.

Your mates are going swimming but you're not a confident swimmer and you're not sure you should go. Do you

1 Lie around on the poolside saying the water's too cold – you're used to swimming in the Med!

2 Give it a miss because what's the point in doing something you're no good at?

3 Stay in your depth and ask them for tips on technique.

4 Take one look at the water and throw up.

Results

Mostly 1: Not knowing makes you feel embarrassed. You need to let go of the idea that showing your ignorance will make other people think less of you.

Mostly 2: Not knowing makes you feel impatient and want to give up. You need to take a deep breath and hang in there.

Mostly 3: You don't mind not knowing and you don't mind other people knowing you don't know. Go to the top of the class – if you aren't there already!

Mostly 4: Not knowing makes you feel anxious and emotional. You need to calm down!

Feeling embarrassed, impatient or anxious when you don't know something is daft because it's unrealistic – of course you don't know everything, you're only human!

Being happy to admit you don't know is sensible, plus it has three whopping brain-boosting bonuses …

Three big bonuses of 'I don't know'

1 *It's good for your self-esteem*

Self-esteem is about accepting yourself just as you are, including all your strengths and weaknesses or, in brain-boosting terms, your knowledge and ignorance.

If you think 'I should know this' when actually you don't, then you aren't accepting yourself as you are. You can end up either having to pretend you know – which will make you feel worried in case someone rumbles you, and humiliated when they do – or you can end up pretending to yourself that you don't care.

2   *It means you can risk a guess because you're not scared of making a mistake*

This is an important part of learning because it's a process of trial and error – you try, you make a mistake, you try again. For example, suppose you've got a spelling test, you keep practising the words until you get them all right, and it's your mistakes that show you which ones you still need to work on.

When it comes to tests and exams it's more important than ever that you aren't scared of having a guess. You might get the answer wrong – but if you'd rather not answer than take the risk then you definitely can't get it right.

3   *If you can't admit you don't know, you can't ask for help*

This isn't just a problem at school, where everyone sometimes needs the teacher to explain things – it can affect your whole life. Look what happened to Carmella.

Carmella

Carmella was shopping with her mum but every five minutes, her mum kept bumping into someone she knew. It was deadly! 'Can I go off on my own?' Carmella pleaded. 'We could meet up at Grindley's in half an hour?'

'Are you sure you can find it?' asked her mum. Yeah, yeah ... whatever!

But after twenty minutes of wandering round the shops, Carmella realised she was lost.

Carmella felt so stupid, she was too embarrassed to ask someone the way, and by the time she accidentally found herself at Grindley's her mum was having kittens.

After that, Carmella didn't want to try going off on her own again and her mum didn't want to let her.

If you're able to ask for help that's good news for other people, because everyone loves being able to help. It's also good for your confidence because it means you've always got back up – you know you won't have to manage all on your own.

You can't learn something you already know and that's why you need lots of ignorance in order to become a champion learner. So don't be afraid of not knowing, brain-boosters – never feel embarrassed, impatient or anxious about it.

Embrace your ignorance now by choosing your Tuesday activity.

Choice of Tuesday activities

❶ Play 20 questions

This is the perfect game for acting on your hunches and learning from your mistakes!

One player thinks of something and tells the others whether it is animal, vegetable or mineral.*

All the others take turns asking questions that can have a yes or no answer, such as 'Is it bigger than a cat? ... Can you eat it? ... Have you got one in your house?'

If no one's guessed the answer after 20 questions, the first player wins. If someone guesses it, it's their turn to think of the next thing.

'Animal' can mean a whole animal, part of an animal or something made from an animal product, like leather or cheese. 'Vegetable' can be a whole plant, part of a plant or something made from a plant, like paper or wood. 'Mineral' is things that aren't animal or vegetable, like water, plastic, glass, stone and metal.

Note: If you get really good, you can mix them. For example, you could say 'vegetable and mineral' for a tin of beans.

❷ Venture into the unknown

Try one food today that you have never tasted before. Make not knowing what it tastes like a reason for trying it, and not a reason for avoiding it. If you always stick to what you know you never learn anything new.

❸ Put your hand up!

Some time today put your hand up and answer a question in class. Ideally, make it something you're not absolutely sure you're right about.

❹ Go on an owl watch

Close your eyes and take three slow breaths to relax your mind. Imagine you're on holiday with your family in a little cottage in the middle of a wood. It's night-time and as you sit around chatting you hear an owl tu-whit-tu-whoo-ing in the trees outside. You want to see the owl.

Go out into the dark garden. At first, you can't see anything in the pitch black. You feel like giving up, but you hold on and gradually your eyes become accustomed to the dark. You can make out the shapes of the trees. There's a flapping, a glimpse of something white. Was it the owl? You go on watching and waiting. Then you see him, sitting on a branch close by, watching you.

To see an owl, you need to be willing to go out into the dark, and be patient. Learning new things is the same – a step in the dark and a wait, until understanding starts to dawn.

➎ The ten-word reminder

Count these words off on your fingers as you say them –

> A mistake is a step on the road to understanding.

Repeat it three times when you wake up, when you go to bed and every time you think of it during the day.

Great learning power is partly a question of attitude, and one way to develop good attitudes is by simply making a statement and repeating it, a bit like brainwashing.

⑥ Do an experiment

Do you know how to make a soap-powered boat? No? Brilliant! Here's your chance to find out.

Cut a boat shape out of cardboard with a notch in the middle at the back. Push a tiny piece of soap into the notch. Gently place the boat on the surface of a bowl of clean water – and watch it go.

Want to know how it works? Ask your teacher or try and find the answer online!

⑦ Great mistakes

Write down a mistake you've made in the past, for example, 'I let my rabbit lick up a blob of margarine.' Then put why it was a mistake – 'He got the runs and I had to clean it up. Yuk!' Finish with what you learnt – 'Rabbits should not eat margarine!'

❽ Have a guess

Answer these three questions – if you don't know the answer, have a guess.

1 What kind of creature is a capercaillie – a bird, a cat or an insect?

2 What kind of food is a bratwurst – a vegetable, a pancake or a sausage?

3 Where would you find your patella – in your leg, in your arm or in your head?

Find out for yourself if you've got them right by looking in a dictionary, online, or asking your teacher / parents / brainy big bro.

❾ 'Run and find out'

The motto of the mongoose family, in Rudyard Kipling's 'The Jungle Book' is 'Run and find out.' Be inspired by the mongooses whenever you don't know something (yes, that is the right plural – it isn't 'mongeese').

To remind yourself, download or copy a picture of a mongoose and stick it on your wall.

⑩ Your 'I' land

Draw an imaginary map of an island in the middle of the sea. This is your 'I' land, so fill it up with words and pics of things you know, like how to read and write and your dad's favourite bikkies and going on holiday to Spain.

Now fill the sea with things you don't know, like who the Prime Minister is (tut, tut!) and how to hang-glide. So much exciting stuff just waiting for you to discover it!

3 WEDNESDAY

Remember, remember

It's not much good being a top explorer if you can never remember where you've been ...

... and it's not much good learning lots of lovely new stuff if you can't remember it either.

It's dead easy remembering things you find interesting and exciting – that's why your mate

Kelly can give you a detailed account of her fave film – all three hours of it – and your bro Stevie can tell you every premiership score since before he was born. That's why Leon shocked everyone at the school general knowledge knockout quiz.

Leon

Leon was bottom of the class in just about everything – he could barely read and write. So when he put his name forward for the school general knowledge knockout quiz, no one thought he was serious.

Imagine their surprise when Leon knocked out one opponent after another and wowed the audience with his awesome memory for random facts from 'What is the world's longest river?'* to 'What kind of animal is a chihuahua?'*

It turned out Leon was a complete quiz nut. He couldn't read so he watched a lot of TV, and he collected facts he found interesting like a jackdaw collecting anything shiny.

In case you're wondering, the answers are the Nile and a very tiny dog.

However, when it comes to remembering things we don't find very interesting, most of us have more of a problem. Test your memory power now by doing Memory Test Number 1.

Memory Test Number 1

Here's a boring old list of ten things which most people wouldn't find particularly fascinating. Read it through a few times, then shut the book and write down as many as you can remember.

T-shirt
key
suitcase
toilet
pineapple
box
France
owl
toast
lawnmower

Results

If you remembered them all first time – skip this chapter and have a day off!

If you couldn't remember them all – read on, because I'm going to give you some top techniques for remembering things.

Three methods using thought processes

The three most common memory-boosting methods are repetition, word association and acronyms.

1   Repetition

This is otherwise known as 'learning by rote' or 'parrot-fashion' and most people use it for remembering things like times tables. Basically, you just keep on repeating what you're trying to remember until it sticks.

It can help to test yourself by writing it down because the act of writing the information seems to help it to go in.

A bit boring, but it does work.

2 *Word association*

This is when you think of a word that sounds like the one you're trying to remember. For example, supposing you want to impress Mr Barclay, the new head teacher, but you keep forgetting his name. Could his 'bark' (Bark-lay) be worse than his bite?

Word association is particularly useful if you want to remember what words mean. Which ones are stalactites and which ones stalagmites? Stalactites hang from the ceiling so they have to hold on '-tite'. Which way round are the Arctic and the Antarctic? Look down to the Antarctic like you would to an ant, and up to the Arctic like you would to an arch.

You can use this technique for anything – say you're choosing takeaway and you can't remember which curry is the hottest, korma or vindaloo … After vindaloo you're in the loo – but korma's calmer.

You can use it to remember the meaning of difficult words as well. For example, 'stingy' means penny-pinching – a stingy person's house would be 'dingy'. 'Truncated' means cut short – like a tree that's been cut down so only a bit of the trunk is left. 'Ingenious' means clever – as 'in genius'.

3   *Acronyms*

Acronyms are useful for learning a set or sequence of things. You make a sentence with words beginning with the same letter as the things you're trying to remember. For example, if you want to remember the planets in our solar system – Mercury, Venus, Earth, Mars, Jupiter, Saturn, Uranus, Neptune and Pluto – you could make up a sentence like *'My very easy method just speeds up naming planets.'*

Do Memory Test 2 and see if this method can work for you.

Memory Test Number 2

Look at this list of ten random things and make an acronym for them – it doesn't matter what order they come in.

bed
leaf
cake
arm
house
elephant
orange
ink
girl
scissors

Go through the list several times, with your sentence in mind – 'a (arm) big (bed) huge (house) giraffe (girl) ...'

Close the book and try to write down as many of the objects as you can, using your acronym as a reminder.

WEDNESDAY

Results

Hopefully better than Test Number 1: unless you were a step ahead and used an acronym for that too!

Using your senses

You remember things better if you experience them with your senses as well as your mind.

Hearing

Putting the things you want to remember into a tune you know makes repetition learning easier.

Smell and taste

This works more for remembering life experiences than schoolwork etc. It worked most famously for a French writer called Marcel Proust. One day, he bit into a madeleine, which was a kind of cake he used to eat when he was little, and his whole past came flooding back to him. He was so blown away by the experience he wrote a thirteen-book epic called *Remembering Things Past*.

Touch

If you hold an object like a pebble or a good luck charm while you're revising for a test and then take it with you in your pocket on the day, feeling it in your fingers again can trigger the memory of the things you revised.

Sight

Creating a visual image of things you want to remember makes it much easier. Say you've heard a new band called Trash and you want to remember their name – make a mental picture of a huge pile of rubbish. If you want to remember your dad's birthday is on the 9th, picture him holding a birthday balloon because a nine looks a bit like a balloon.

53

The method of loci

The method all champion memorizers use is called 'the method of loci'. Loci means *locations* and is pronounced *low-key* – so if you want to remember that, look down low and see a key! This is the method: you place all the things you want to remember along an imaginary journey around a familiar place, such as your house.

This method takes a bit longer but once it's done, the memory thing is sorted. No more boring repetitions. And the more you do it, the more natural it becomes for you. Try it now with Memory Test Number 3.

Memory Test Number 3

Here is a list of ten random things – again!

bucket
crocodile
sandwich
bike
peanut
TV
flower
spider
pencil
wig

Go on an imaginary journey through your house or garden, encountering each of the objects in turn. Make them bigger or more colourful than they really would be. Let some of them be obstacles that you have to get past, because that will help to fix them in your mind. Repeat the journey several times in your mind's eye.

Close the book, do the journey again and write down all the items you remember as you come to them.

Results

10 out of 10: not surprising – as memory methods go this one's the daddy!

More than you got in Tests 1 and 2: shows it's worth working at.

Same or less than in the other tests: at least it was more fun, right?

Putting it all together

You can mix and match these memory techniques, so be creative! Supposing you've managed to learn all the eight times table by heart except you keep forgetting seven times eight is fifty-six.

Seven sounds like *Devon*, which is where they make clotted cream.

Times sounds like a newspaper.

Eight sounds like a *gate*.

Is sounds like *fizz*.

Fifty sounds like *shifty* and

Six sounds like *fix*.

Put it together in an imaginary walk from your house to the street. You go out the door and yuk! You've put your foot in a big puddle of *Devon* cream! A super-size *Times* newspaper is lying on the path so you wipe your foot on it. You go through the *gate*. There's a gigantic glass full of *fizzy* lemonade in the way so you have to squeeze round it. When you get through you see some *shifty* looking lads. Now you're in a *fix*!

Everyone can have a good memory – it isn't just down to luck. There are lots of methods you can use to get your memory into tip-top condition, so pick a Wednesday activity now – before you forget!

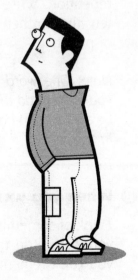

Choice of Wednesday activities

❶ A word a day ...

Flick through the dictionary and choose a word you didn't know the meaning of before, such as 'hirsute' or 'prattle'.

Make a word association to help you remember the meaning. Hirsute means hairy and it sounds like 'hair suit'. Prattle means meaningless chatter or baby-talk, and it sounds like 'rattle'.

If you can't think of a word-association, learn it by repetition. Write down the word and its meaning ten times, then test yourself on a new piece of paper.

Note: One word isn't much but if you were to do this every day you'd be a total brain-box in no time at all. Imagine!

❷ When you were little

Think of something you used to love eating when you were little that you haven't had for ages. If you can't remember, ask your mum. Maybe you loved soft boiled egg and soldiers, or mushy cornflakes or sherbet dippers.

Eat some today. Take your time. See if the experience triggers memories from your past.

❸ Make some visuals

Supposing your mate was moving to Melrose and you wanted to remember and tell your mum after school. You could make a mental picture of a nose (smell) and a flower (rose) and that would remind you of the name – Melrose.

Look at these five place names and think of a visual image for each one that might help you remember it.

Greenham   Southfield   Braintree
Swansea   Newcastle

Do a cartoon sketch of each one to reinforce the image.

❹ Play 'What's missing?'

In this game, one person gathers 10–15 objects on a tray and brings it in for the other players to look at. After a few minutes, he or she takes the tray outside, removes one object and comes back.

The first player to guess what's missing makes the next display.

Note: For an interesting experiment, let the players handle the objects instead of just looking. See if that helps them to spot what's missing quicker.

❺ Animals and Neighbours

'Neighbours, everybody needs good neighbours ...' You know the tune. Change the words, so it says something you want to remember.

It could be schoolwork facts –

'Animals are divided into two groups, vertebrates and then invertebrates, and the reason why is this ... Vertebrates, they're the kind that have a backbone, but those invertebrates don't have one at all ...'

Or it could be any random thing you don't want to forget –

'01 76592 8347 that's the number for Colleen ...'

Note: If you don't know the Neighbours theme tune or you can't stand it, choose a different one that you like.

❻ Interesting facts

Learn one interesting new fact today. Think of something you'd like to know, such as 'who was the first man to walk on the moon?'* and either ask your teacher, look it up in an encyclopaedia or go to Google and type in the key words.

Choose one of the methods in this chapter to help you remember it.

*It was Neil Armstrong, in case you're wondering.

❼ Don't look down!

When you get stuck trying to remember things in tests and exams, you tend to look down, but research suggests you might remember better if you looked up.

Give it a try if you have a test at school today. If you don't, get your mum or dad to ask you questions you should know the answer to, and try looking up when you get stuck.

I'm not saying this will work – but it could be interesting!

 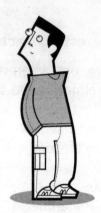

❽ Remembering things at school

Think of a food, an animal, a piece of furniture, a container, a plant, an article of clothing and a toy. Write them down.

Take an imaginary walk from the front gate of your school into your classroom, meeting all your objects along the way, using the 'method of loci'.

Cover up your list and repeat your imaginary walk, writing down each object as you come to it.

➒ 'I packed my bag ...'

Memory games are great practice as well as being good fun. Try this one with your family or friends.

The first player says, 'I packed my bag and in it I put ...' Then they make something up, say '... a peach'. The second player repeats that and adds something of their own, making it as weird and outrageous as they like. 'I packed my bag and in it I put a peach ... and a sabre-toothed tiger.'

The game continues with everyone taking turns repeating the list and adding something new. If anyone gets stuck, they're out, and the next player takes their turn, until finally there's just one super-champion-memorizer left.

➓ Try and try again

Write down as many memory tricks as you can remember from this chapter, without re-reading it.

Check and see what you've missed – then shut the book and try again!

4 THURSDAY

A healthy mind in a healthy body

Nearly 2000 years ago, in ancient Rome, a v. famous writer called Juvenal said a v. famous thing: *Mens sana in corpore sano* – 'a healthy mind in a healthy body'. In more recent times, we seem to have forgotten that the brain is actually part of the body, with the same needs as the rest of it, so if we want our brains to work brilliantly we need to look after their physical needs as well as just shovelling in facts and information.

What does your body need to keep it in tip-top condition? Healthy food, water, sleep and exercise. Your brain says, 'Yes please – I'll have some of that!'

Healthy food

Food gives you energy and at least 20 per cent of all the energy that comes from your food is needed to power your brain. Imagine that – a fifth of every choccy bar and apple and sandwich you eat. Considering your brain is only about the size of a grapefruit, that's a lot!

The amount of energy your brain is using right now could power a lightbulb ...

All that energy is what makes your head get hot and it's why, if you want to keep warm on a cold day, the best way is to wear a hat and keep the heat in.

Food is brain-fuel. You wouldn't expect a car to run on empty, and neither will your brain. So the first rule of brain fuel is –

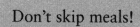

Don't skip meals!

Especially, don't skip breakfast because your brain's already been fasting all night so eating something when you get out of bed is v. important.

There's lots of evidence that brains don't work so well without brekkie – if you dash out of the house with an empty stomach you're much more likely to have an accident; you're less likely to do well in tests and you'll find it harder to concentrate in class. Fact!

So that's one thing – your brain needs regular meals and little snacks to keep it ticking over nicely. The other thing to think about is the quality of the fuel you're putting in.

We all know about healthy eating, and what's good for your body is good for your brain, so the second rule of brain-fuel is –

Have a healthy diet!

The key is balance and variety – if you live on burgers and chips you're only getting a narrow range of nutrients, so you need to swap some fries for fruit and veg.

The science is complicated, but our bodies are perfectly adapted to digest things that grow naturally so on the whole, the nearer a food is to the natural state it was grown in the better. For example, a banana is better than a biscuit, a boiled potato is better than a plate of oven chips; a glass of milk is better than a milk-shake; and a slice of turkey is better than a twizzler.

THURSDAY

Water

How much water do you drink? Experts say we should all be drinking at least eight glasses of water every day! If you do a lot of sport, you may even need more. Ditto if the weather's hot.

You're doing a quick calculation, right? You're thinking, I'm OK – I have a drink before I go to school and one at break-time and one at dinner time ... Sorry! It's only water that counts. Fruit juice, fizzy drinks, tea and coffee may quench your thirst for a while but they are diuretics, which is a fancy way of saying they make you pee. So they don't really help you keep your fluid levels up.

Not drinking enough water can cause headaches, drowsiness and difficulty concentrating.

Sleep

If you think that bedtimes are for babies, your brain does not agree! Going to bed at the same time every night, at least on weekdays, and getting up at the same time in the morning is the best way to ensure you get a good night's sleep – and if you don't get enough sleep your brain will feel tired the next day just like your body.

The biggest enemy of bedtime is TV and computer games. For one thing, they're so hard to switch off – it tends to get later and later as you just try one more level or wait for the end of the programme. For another thing, they excite your brain rather than calming it down, and that means it's harder to go to sleep once you do finally turn your light off.

Fatima

Fatima's teacher was worried because she wasn't doing as well as she used to and she always seemed tired and irritable. When he asked her if anything had happened to upset her, she bit his head off!

So he had a chat with Fatima's parents. He asked them whether Fatima was getting enough sleep. They said yes, she always went up to bed no problems. But that conversation got them thinking ...

Instead of just assuming that Fatima went straight to sleep when she went to bed, they decided to check up on her. Sure enough, they found that she had been watching TV – with the sound turned right down – until nearly midnight every night.

They took the TV out of her room and said she could have it back when her teacher was happy that her work and behaviour were back to normal. Within a few weeks, they were – and Fatima was feeling so much better that she never needed to be reminded again about switching her telly off at night.

The best thing is to make the half hour before you turn your light off unwind-time. Reading, drawing, writing your diary, listening to an audiobook or some gentle music – these are great ways of calming your body and mind and preparing yourself for sleep. It's also a good idea to have a light snack before you clean your teeth, because you won't sleep so well if you go to bed hungry.

Exercise

Exercise is great for your whole body, even the bits you may not be aware of exercising, like your heart and lungs, your digestion and yes, your brain. Scientists have shown that exercise actually makes brains grow bigger!

It also has the added bonus of improving your mood, putting you in a more positive frame of mind, and that's a big boost for your thinking-skills.

Next time you're tempted to skip breakfast, or not bother to have a glass of water, or play computer games all night, or be a couch potato – remember it isn't just your body that's getting a raw deal – your brain is as well.

Your brain can't do the biz if it's tired, dried out and hungry, so get a healthy mind in a healthy body now by choosing your Thursday activity.

Choice of Thursday activities

❶ Make a breakfast menu

Look through your kitchen cupboards and get creative! Make up a menu of five different breakfasts you could have. 'Like, how?' I hear you splutter. 'We've only got one measly packet of Weetabix!'

Well let me see ... Weetabix and sultanas, Weetabix and yoghurt, Weetabix and orange juice instead of milk, Weetabix spread with butter and jam like toast, Weetabix with warm milk, Weetabix and chopped banana ... I said be creative!

Note: Remember to include a drink. Orange juice is particularly good because it helps your body absorb iron in the food.

❷ Head, shoulders, knees and toes

If you don't know this movement-and-music game, ask your teacher / mum and dad / mates about it – and then do it!

Note: Any dance routine will do if you prefer to copy from a music video, or find someone with a dance mat.

❸ Drink water

Start your day with a glass of water when you get up. Then have a drink whenever you normally would throughout the day, but make it water.

End the day with a lovely glass of water when you go to bed.

Note: If you really want fizzy drinks / fruit juice / tea, have them as well as water, but not instead.

❹ Couch potato plus

If you normally watch TV in the evening, instead of flicking the channels during the ad breaks, run up and down the stairs three times. That way, the more you watch, the more exercise you do!

If you don't watch TV, do this anyway at least four times during the evening.

If you live in a flat or bungalow and haven't got any stairs, run on the spot for one minute instead.

THURSDAY ACTIVITIES

❺ Bliss out

Bliss out at bedtime by giving yourself some quality unwind-time. Make a light snack – milk, bananas and peanuts are all particularly good for soothing and relaxing your mind. Get pillows and cushions to create a cosy nest, and kick back with a good book or magazine, an audiobook or some mellow sounds for half an hour before you switch your light off.

❻ Eat, drink ... and jot it down

At the end of the day, think back and make a list of all the things you've had to eat and drink since you woke up, including snacks. Most of the time, we just guzzle and don't think about it – making a record is a way of being more food-aware.

Ask yourself, 'Am I drinking enough water?' and 'Am I getting a good variety of foods?' Think about one way you might have had a healthier day, diet-wise.

❼ Get active

Do an extra half-hour of any physical activity today – walking, cycling, skateboarding, having a kick-around, shooting some hoops ... Anything you fancy, because as the old saying goes, 'A bit of what you fancy does you good.'

❽ Eat a carrot!

Carrots contain betacarotene which is good for your brain-power – plus they make a lovely crunchy snack.

If you don't like carrots, have some sunflower seeds instead because they've got vitamin E, or any fruit for the vitamin C, or a nice glass of milk for the omega-3s – they're all brilliant brain-foods!

❾ Have a stretch

Lock your fingers together, turn your palms outwards, and push your ·hands up above your head as you breathe in. Drop your hands back into your lap as you breathe out.

A good stretch gets your body moving and sends a burst of extra oxygen to your brain.

⑩ Relax!

Lie down on your back with your feet hip width apart and your hands facing upwards a bit out from your body. As you breathe in, imagine you're drawing all the tension up out of your feet, and as you breathe out again imagine sending warmth and relaxation back down to replace it.

Gradually work your way up through your body, breathing the tension away from your legs, hips, stomach, chest, hands, arms, shoulders, neck, and head, and sending warmth and relaxation back on the out breath.

Mmmmm ... nice!

Note: Try this as a gorgeous way of dozing off to sleep at bedtime.

5 FRIDAY

Give your brain a break

When it comes to brain work, more isn't always better. It's no good filling up your head with facts and information all day long if you don't leave time for understanding and ideas to come. Now and then, you need to stop the slog and give your brain a break.

Are you working your brain too hard? Do the quiz and find out.

Quiz

You and your mates are talking about a new band over lunch and none of you can remember the lead singer's name. Do you

1   Sit there with your head in your hands for the rest of lunchtime muttering, 'I can get this ... I know I can ...'

2   Give up and talk about something else.

3   Talk about something else but keep the question in the back of your mind.

You've been doing your maths homework and now you're stuck. Do you

1   Keep poring over it, refusing to budge even when your mum calls you downstairs for supper.

2   Feed it to the dog.

3   Watch 'Neighbours' and go back to it.

You're supposed to be coming up with an idea for a story and you can't think of anything. Do you

1 Get cross with yourself and try to force an idea to come even though your mind's gone totally blank.

2 Distract everyone else by writing silly notes about your teacher.

3 Do a doodle on your rough book and see if any ideas come.

You're doing a ten-question test and you're stuck on Question three. Do you

1 Keep trying to think of the answer even though time's running out.

2 Cross the whole test out and put, 'Who do you think I am, Einstein?'

3 Push on with the rest of the test and come back to it when you've answered all the other questions.

Results

Mostly 1: You're a hard task master – no wonder your brain's refusing to work.

Mostly 2: You're a complete pushover – your brain needs a tea-break, not a month in the Seychelles!

Mostly 3: You're the boss – you keep your brain busy but give it the space it needs to deliver the goods.

Giving your brain a break when you get stuck isn't about switching off and forgetting all about the problem – it's about focusing on something else for a short time while keeping the problem in the back of your mind.

Did you ever play 'Grandmother's Footsteps' when you were little? One person turns to face the wall and all the others stand in a line a long way behind him. They try to creep up on the person facing the wall, but he can turn round at any moment, and if he sees anyone actually moving, that person has to go back to the start line.

Well, brain-breaks are like that. You're looking away, but you stay alert to what's going on in the back of your mind – and when you sense that the information you're looking for is on the move, you turn and pounce!

This method is super-efficient in three big brain functions – remembering, understanding and getting new ideas.

Remembering

Everyone's had this experience. You're trying to remember something, maybe a name or a date or an interesting fact … it's on the tip of your tongue … you're thinking really hard … you're rubbing your forehead …

Nope, it's just no good, it isn't coming! You stop trying so hard and then … it suddenly pops into your head all by itself.

Understanding

This is common too. Your teacher's been explaining about longshore drift or apostrophes or fractions and you're just not getting it … you're so glad when break-time comes.

Then when you come back to class and start again, suddenly, you get it. Ah-ha – so that's what she was talking about!

Getting new ideas

A big study into 120 business directors found that most of them got their best ideas lying in the bath, walking the dog or sitting on the beach. This is true! The study concluded, 'Ideas tend to come to us away from work because this is the time when we allow our minds to drift and dream.'

The most famous example of this is probably Archimedes, who actually had his ah-ha moment in the bath.

Archimedes

The king of Syracuse wanted a golden crown, so he gave a lump of gold to the royal goldsmith and asked him to make a crown with it. The goldsmith made the crown ... but the king was suspicious.

Although the crown weighed exactly the same amount as the lump of gold, he thought the goldsmith might have cheated by using some silver in it instead and keeping the spare gold for himself. He asked Archimedes to find out if it was true.

Archimedes racked his brains but he couldn't think of a way of testing whether the goldsmith had melted some silver into the gold (this was hundreds of years ago, so he couldn't just pop down to his local forensic laboratory).

In his frustration, he decided to go to the baths and forget about the problem for a bit. As he jumped in the bath, some water sloshed out. 'Eureka!' cried Archimedes (that's probably Greek for 'ah-ha!').

He hadn't been able to work it out by thinking – but seeing the water being displaced by his body gave him an idea. He put the crown in a jar filled to the brim with water and measured the amount that overflowed. Then he did the same with the lump of gold that weighed the same as the crown. Less water overflowed so then he knew the crown wasn't pure gold – and the goldsmith was busted!

Explanation: Things have different densities, which means they can weigh the same but take up more or less room – like a kilo of bread takes up more room than a kilo of cheese

If you keep bashing your head against a brick wall, your brain doesn't like it. So whenever you feel stuck, stop. Take some time out. If you're at school, you might have to limit it to a few moments looking out the window or a doodle in your rough book, but at home you can take a bit more time.

Try lots of different brain-refreshers. Choose one now from the Friday activities.

Choice of Friday activities

❶ Do a doodle

Do you find yourself scribbling in the margin when you can't think of any ideas? It's nature's way of distracting your mind just a little bit, helping you to relax mentally and allow ideas to come or information to sink in.

Do a doodle, noticing what happens to your brain. There are the lines, there are the colours, not going anywhere in particular, just meandering along. Soothing, isn't it?

❷ Have a daydream

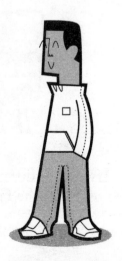

A little daydream is like playtime for your brain, and you can have one any time you like, no need to wait until they come along.

Start one off by imagining you're meeting one of your personal heroes or villains – a soapstar maybe, a rugby player or a politician. Where are you? What do you say to them? What do they say to you? How are you feeling?

'I'm at this concert in Hyde Park. There are people everywhere and the band's playing really loud, and suddenly I see Jacqueline Wilson in the crowd, with all her silver rings ...'

Warning: Daydreaming is seriously enjoyable so you might get carried away. If you happen to start a particularly brilliant one at school, press pause and go back to it later.

❸ Be a tree*

This exercise stops you thinking about anything else because if your mind wanders you fall over!

Stand straight and tall with your feet together, shoulders back and arms by your sides. Take a few breaths while you relax into the position.

Find a spot to focus on just in front of you on the ground, and keep looking at it – this is the important bit because the key to success is in the concentration. Then shift your weight on to your left foot and lift your right foot off the ground, placing it on the inside of your left knee. Bring your hands together in front of your chest as if you're praying.

Try to hold the position while you count to five. Repeat it standing on the other foot.

*This is based on a yoga position called 'the tree'.

❹ Read a story

This is a longer brain-break but v. useful for when you're stuck with bigger problems like family or friends stuff – say, your mates want you to join in with them when they have a smoke, or your sister keeps telling tales.

If your brain's got stuck into worry, worry, worry and no solutions are coming, distract it with other people's problems and challenges, and let other people's solutions inspire you.

❺ Counting and breathing

Breathe in slowly, counting in your head, 1001, 1002, 1003 ... As you breathe out again, count 1004, 1005, 1006 ...

Do this for ten breaths, folding one finger into your palm after each one so you don't forget how many you've done.

Counting and breathing is a way taking your mind off things for a few moments because you can't think about two things at once.

❻ Tune in to music

The patterns in music are very restful for your brain and that's why lots of people like listening to music while they work. You can't do that at school, but try running through a song in your head if you feel tense or stuck with your work today.

❼ Play Grandmother's Footsteps

If you've got some younger kids around or if your mates are up for a laugh you could do this in real life, but in your memory or imagination is just as good.

Close your eyes and really picture it. You're standing in front of the wall, you turn and look at the line, you're turning away, you're looking at the wall. Notice the colour of the wall – is it made of bricks or concrete or stones? Is there any moss on it, or graffiti?

How does it feel to be looking at the wall but alert for any movement going on behind you? That tension is the same as when you're holding a question in the back of your mind – 'What was that lead singer's name?' – and giving the answer time to creep up on you.

❽ Do a mini meditation

Maybe the word 'meditation' makes you think of people sitting cross-legged with their eyes shut for hours, but it's really just about clearing your mind by letting go of all your thoughts and worries.

You do it all the time without noticing, like when something catches your eye and every other thought goes out of your head for a few moments.

Do it consciously today three times. Think, 'I need a break' – look at the first thing you see – really look. Be absorbed in its colours and shapes, and for just a minute let everything else go out of your mind.

❾ Make a mandala

Mandalas are geometrical patterns based around a circle. Start with a circle (draw round a tumbler or use compasses if your free-hand circles look more like sausages).

Put a square inside or outside the circle – or both – you can make your own rules. If you prefer, put a triangle inside, or two triangles.

FRIDAY ACTIVITIES

Play with the basic shapes building up your own design around a central point. The act of creating symmetrical shapes is a great brain-soother and when you've finished, simply looking at them can have the same effect.

Note: If you like art, try colouring them in. Focusing on colours is a great brain-soother too.

⑩ Sakaraka!

Make up a nonsense word like sakaraka or fodapi – just a mix of sounds that don't mean anything or remind you of any real words.

Repeat your nonsense word under your breath for a few minutes, noticing what happens to your brain.

This is a great way to still your mind because your brain is flummoxed – it's listening, but it simply can't make any sense of what you're saying.

6 SATURDAY

Pick other people's brains

Information is coming at you all the time from other people – teachers, family and friends, writers of books and websites, TV and radio programme-makers … It's up to you how you deal with it, and you've got three choices.

1 *Believe everything*

Advantage – You don't have to bother to think about things.

Disadvantage – You're *sooooo* gullible!

2 *Believe nothing*

Advantage – You don't have to bother etc.

Disadvantage – You're never going to learn anything.

3 *Test everything and make your own mind up what you think of it*

Advantage – You're making the most of all the information available to you, plus you're in control.

Disadvantage – It takes more effort.

Obviously, brain boosters choose option three, and their first task is to try and spot whether the information being given is a fact or an opinion. Do the facts-and-opinions sorter and see how good you are at this.

The facts-and-opinions sorter

Which of these statements express factual information (whether it's correct or not) and which are the speaker's opinion?

F O

1 'Lord of the Rings' is a fantastic film. ☐ ☐

2 After-school tennis is on Wednesdays. ☐ ☐

3 There are 26 bones in the human foot. ☐ ☐

4 Classical music is boring. ☐ ☐

5 Most people watch too much TV. ☐ ☐

6 Right now, I am doing the facts-and-opinions sorter. ☐ ☐

7 The facts-and-opinions sorter is too easy. ☐ ☐

F O

8 Shakespeare is the best writer in the English language. ☐ ☐

9 Cows have one stomach with four compartments. ☐ ☐

10 The Harry Potter books are written by J K Rowling. ☐ ☐

Results

1, 4, 5, 7 **and** *8* are all opinions. Even commonly held opinions like Shakespeare being the best writer are still just opinions. Who says, and where's the proof?

2, 3, 6, 9 **and** *10* are factual statements because you can prove whether they are right or wrong.

When it comes to facts, the rule is … check!

The only facts you can be one hundred per cent sure about are things you know for yourself, such as 'There are 27 kids in my class' and 'My birthday is the sixth of June'. With second-hand facts you have to decide for yourself whether to believe them or not, and that will depend on where they came from.

You can be pretty confident about facts from reliable sources such as

- Teachers

- Text books

- Major websites like www.bbc.co.uk

- Family and friends on subjects they know about – for example, your taxi-driver dad giving directions to the swimming pool

But you might want to use reliable sources to check anything you get from unreliable ones such as

- Small websites

- The media

- Family and friends on subjects they don't know about – your dizzy mate Millie on just about anything, for example!

When it comes to opinions, the rule is ... respect!

Everyone is entitled to their own opinion. You might not agree with them, but you should respect their right to think the way they do, and claim your own right to think the way you do. See if you've got it by doing the Opinions Quiz.

The Opinions Quiz

You've just seen the latest blockbuster movie with your mates. They're raving about it, but you slept through most of the second half. Do you

1   Say it was a load of rubbish and they're all idiots.

2   Ask them what they liked so much about it.

3   Think there must be something wrong with you.

A TV documentary says rabies might be coming to Britain. Do you

1 Dismiss the idea out of hand.

2 See what your mum and dad think about it.

3 Make a will.

Your class has a debate on 'Do we need the monarchy?' You think Yes but most people vote No. Do you

1 Not bother to argue – what's the point in debates?

2 Listen to both sides.

3 Take all your royal posters down as soon as you get home.

Your grandpa says life was better before TV. Do you

1   Stifle a yawn.

2   Try to imagine it.

3   Feel hard done by that you weren't born 50 years ago.

Results

Mostly 1: Your opinions are set in stone – so no chance of learning and growing there then!

Mostly 2: You've got your own views but you're willing to listen to other people's – go brain booster!

Mostly 3: Your opinions are as shaky as a jelly on a motor bike.

If you want to be open to maximum learning, respect other people's opinions even if you don't agree with them and view your own as a work-in-progress. Be prepared to stand your ground, but also be prepared to be persuaded. Develop your ideas through talking and listening.

Talking and listening

In conversation, we remember about 20% of what we hear but 80% of what we say. That's why it's important to express your point of view and not just sit and listen.

But don't think of discussions as a competition that has to result in winners and losers; think of them as an exchange of ideas from which everyone can benefit. Offer your views, don't ram them down people's throats, because as soon as someone gets aggressive in an argument the other side has to fight or cave in, and either way the chance to learn from each other is lost.

It helps if you back up your ideas with reasons – 'We should recycle because we're running out of space for landfill sites …' If you get in the habit of doing this it makes your argument more convincing and it also shows you where your reasons are a bit thin on the ground.

Almost all of the information we get comes through other people so if you give your brain a good book, an interesting programme or a lively conversation, it feels like it's in a sweetie shop!

Being interested in what people say, being discerning, and making your own contribution – that's how to make the best of your biggest learning resource: other people. Start now by choosing your Saturday activity.

Choice of Saturday activities

❶ Be on the lookout

Notice the things people say to you today, and ask 'Is that a fact or an opinion?' Be on the lookout for one fact and one opinion that you can record in your notebook.

❷ Write a review

Think of a book, film or TV show you've seen recently and start with the factual details – title, author / stars / channel, date of review.

Now write your opinions about it, remembering to support them with evidence. 'It wasn't as good as his last book because the main character was a bit boring ...'

❸ Sort your sources

Write down a question – anything you would like to know. For example, 'How do planes stay up?' or 'Does Mel fancy me?'

List all the people who might have the information you need, including written sources. Put them in order of reliability starting with the one you can trust most.

SATURDAY ACTIVITIES

Good learning isn't just about looking for information – it's also about choosing the best places to look.

❹ True or false?

Here are three 'facts' that might be true but they might not.

1 Peanuts grow under the ground.

2 Rabbits eat their own poo.

3 An egg will sink in fresh water but float in very salty water.

Think of three ways you could check each fact – then go ahead and do one.

❺ Talk and listen

Ask your mum / dad / sis / bro / mate what's the best book they've ever read. Ask them what they particularly liked about it. Tell them your best book ever, and say why you loved it.

Note: If your family and friends aren't into reading, go for a favourite film or TV show instead.

➏ Repeat this reminder ...

Everyone's entitled to their own opinion but it's easy to forget that. Get the idea firmly lodged in your brain by repeating this reminder three times when you wake up, three times at dinner time and three times when you go to bed.

It's OK for me to disagree with you

It's OK for you to disagree with me

➐ Track an opinion

To see how your opinions develop and grow, write down your fave band or singer and put the reasons why you love them. Then write down a band or singer you used to love, and the reasons why you've gone off them.

➑ Show me

Visit www.show.me.uk and spend ten minutes exploring the info, games and activities they've got on offer.

Check out the show-and-tell pages. Have you got anything you could share?

❾ Express yourself

Take every opportunity today to express an opinion. If you don't like the new breakfast cereal with marshmallow pieces, say so! If you think the new game show is wicked, say so!

And remember –

- Give your reasons – 'I find it a bit too sweet ...', 'I love the host, he's hilarious!'

- Listen to other people's opinions – Don't worry if they disagree with you.

❿ Make a feedback sandwich

you look great...
not sure about the shorts...
but I love that new top!

One ace way of expressing a negative opinion without getting someone's back up is by sandwiching it between two positive comments.

Watch out for a chance to make a feedback sandwich today.

7 SUNDAY

Play!

Most of the learning you do in school involves facts, skills and information, and the challenge for your brain is to understand and remember things. You're probably dead good at this because you get so much practice. Do the Comprehension Test and see.

The Comprehension Test

Read the paragraph and answer the questions.

Faye and Suze wanted to get something nice to wear for the school disco. They went to 'Funky' in the mall because it had a great selection of cool clothes and wasn't too expensive. Faye got a green top with sparkles but Suze couldn't find anything she liked, so they went to the café next door to plan where to go next.

Questions

1 Where did Faye and Suze go to look for clothes?

2 What were their two reasons for choosing that shop?

3 What did Faye buy?

4 Where was the café?

5 Why did they need new clothes in the first place?

Answers

1 'Funky'

2 It had a good selection and wasn't expensive.

3 Green top with sparkles.

4 Next door to 'Funky'.

5 For the school disco.

Leisure activities like computer games and TV are like most of your schoolwork in that the information and images are given, and all you have to do is understand and remember them.

This kind of learning develops your powers of reason and observation, but leaves nothing to your imagination – and the wonderful world of the imagination is where your brain feels free to have adventures and play.

'But I haven't got any imagination!' I hear you wail. Hmm ... worrying! Do the 'Picture this' quiz and see if it's true – could your brain have forgotten how to play?

The 'Picture this' quiz

Read the paragraphs, picture the scene and make up the answers (it's no good looking for them in the paragraphs!)

As soon as Hamish got the message he ran down through the field behind his house, with Wolfie at his heels. They came to the stile at the bottom, climbed over, and entered the woods.

> *The path dipped steeply down towards the river.*
> *They could hear the water nearby, and the*
> *rustling of the leaves. They dived into the*
> *undergrowth and crawled into the den. No one*
> *else was there yet.*

Questions

1   How does the message come?

2   What time of day or night is it?

3   How big is Wolfie?

4   Is the stile new or rickety?

5   Are the woods dense and dark or sparse and
sun-dappled/moonlit?

Answers

This quiz is different from the first one because
you haven't been given much info at all – you
have to fill in the gaps for yourself, using your
imagination. That means there are *no right or
wrong answers* – how fantastic is that?!

Doing what comes naturally ... plus

Using your imagination comes naturally all the time, for example

- You automatically make pictures in your mind of everything you read or hear.

- In idle moments, you find yourself daydreaming.

- You imagine the future every time you make decisions and set goals.

- You develop social skills by imagining what it's like to be another person.

Everyone's got a great imagination – but you can make it even stronger by using it deliberately and playfully. And that's not only good fun, it's great brain-boosting too.

Here are three ways that using your imagination leads to gold-star learning –

1 *It gets you thinking independently*

Your imagination is completely unique. If you were to ask a thousand people to imagine a garden, for example, none of them would come up with the same images.

2 *It's a way of learning from experience*

Story-making, daydreaming, role-playing ...
these are all ways of gaining experience in
your imagination that you might not be able
to get in real life.

3 *It encourages you to experiment*

'What is real was once imagined.' That's a
quote from William Blake, who invented his
own printing method and wrote books full of
poems and pics that are still famous nearly
200 years after his death. What a brain-
boosting hero!

All great inventors use their imagination – first
to dream up their ideas and then to devise
ways of testing them out.

The best learners use all their learning powers,
including the amazing power of the imagination.

How can you build up your imaginative powers?
Play! Play is the natural element for your
imagination, just like water is the natural element
for fish. Playing gives your imagination freedom
to move, to explore and to help you achieve.

Start playing now by choosing some Sunday fun and games.

Sunday fun and games

❶ Picture-strip your life

This is about imagining your ideal future. Write down lots of things you want to happen in your future, such as 'Be an astronaut' and 'Have my own horse'.

Select five things from your wish list and put them in order, starting with some that might happen soon and some way ahead in the future.

Divide a piece of paper into six squares and in the first one draw a pic of yourself right now. Then fill in the other five squares with the picture story of your ideal life.

Note: Remember you can use all the lovely features of a picture strip – captions, labels, speech bubbles, think bubbles, 'Kerpow!'s ...

❷ What's the story?

Choose one of the storylines in your fave soap or drama series – maybe one of the characters has stolen some money, for example. Write a sentence describing the situation – 'Frankie has taken £50 from the shop till.'

Think of three different ways the plot might develop, and write a sentence for each ... 'He might feel guilty and fess up', 'He might think he's got away with it and do it again', 'Mrs Smith might have seen him do it' ...

Choose one of them and write three sentences describing what might happen next –

'Mrs Smith tries to blackmail him ... He's broke, so she tries to make him do things for her, like mow the lawn ... While he's in her house, he tampers with the electrics, so when she turns the kettle on, kaboom!'

Making up stories is easy and fun, plus it's a great workout for your imagination.

❸ Go people-watching

Take a few moments when you're out and about today to pause and notice the people around you.

SUNDAY FUN AND GAMES

Say you're at the park and there's a young mum there with a baby, or two older kids kicking a ball. Imagine their lives – make up their stories. Maybe the young mum has been abandoned by her baby's father, or maybe she lives in a leafy street with him and they're sooooo in love. Maybe the kids with the ball are mates now though they used to be enemies. What happened to make them stop hating each other?

Note: This is fab fun to do with a mate, but be careful not to stare and remember to keep your voices down!

❹ The magic garden

Take a few moments to close your eyes and imagine you're in a garden. Stroll around. What can you see? Are there lots of flowers and trees? Or grass – a football field or tennis court maybe? Is there any water in the garden? Any play equipment such as a trampoline or aerial walkway?

This garden is magic because nobody else in the entire world can see it except you.

Before it disappears, draw a map or picture of it, or write a description or poem.

❺ Think outside the box

Take any three household objects and think of a new use for them. A shoe ... that could be an attractive plant pot! A coffee table ... that could be a spiders' social club ...

Make some drawings of your ideas.

❻ Play consequences

This is a story-making game. You need two or more players, a piece of paper each and a pen.

Everyone starts by writing the name of a boy or man at the top of their piece of paper. It can be someone real like the Prime Minister or fictional like Harry Potter. Then you fold the paper over to conceal the name and pass it on to the person next to you.

SUNDAY FUN AND GAMES

Next, everyone writes 'met' and the name of a girl or woman. They fold the paper down again to hide what they've written, and pass it on.

After that, you write and hide the place where they met, pass it on, then 'He said ...', then 'She said ...' then 'The consequence was ...' Finally, you pass the papers on again, unfold them, and read the whole story out loud. It'll probably be pretty weird!

Our head teacher...

Met Marge Simpson ...

at the Swings in Coronation Park ...

he said, 'Do you like my Bad Boyz T-shirt?' ...

she said, 'That's enough of your cheek!' ...

and the consequence was they decided to run away together

❼ Be someone else

Copying someone's body language is a great way to imagine how it feels to be someone else. Do it discreetly though – it could also be a great way of annoying people and making yourself unpopular.

The safest way is to copy TV presenters in the privacy of your own living room. Notice their gestures, the way they stand and move, their facial expressions. See how it feels to be them by copying what they do. Lots of writers use this technique to 'get into character' but anyone can use it to have new experiences in their imagination that they can't have in real life.

❽ Read a story

Stories are like magic. They are created in the writer's imagination but they come to life through yours. You make the pictures, feelings and sensations, from simple marks on the page. You bring the characters and settings into glorious colour in your mind's eye.

Use your imagination today by reading a piece of fiction. Feel the magic!

❾ Take a line for a walk

On a plain piece of paper, using the hand you don't normally draw with, start making a line and keep going. Your line can loop and weave wherever you like, but keep the pen on the paper until you feel you've done enough.

Now sit back and look at your doodle. Can you see any pictures in it ... a house, a face, a stormy sea? Use coloured pens or pencils to pick out the images you can see.

❿ Have a cocktail party!

This is fun, creative and hopefully tasty too! Invite some mates round and ask them to bring a bottle of fizzy drink or fruit juice, plus one piece of fruit. You provide a tin of coconut milk, some cherries and cocktail umbrellas, and a few nibbles.

Take turns creating cocktails by mixing two or three ingredients in a jug and pouring it into some small glasses for everyone to try. Playing around and experimenting is your brain's most favourite way of finding out what works ... and what doesn't!

The Sunday Bonus

Yay – you did it! You completed a whole week of brilliant brain-boosting! Remember to buy yourself a little gift and wrap it up for a big celebration at the end if you're going for the full ten weeks.

Going for the full ten weeks

I highly recommend it! Doing a little every day will help you to start a brain-boosting habit, so adventurousness, confidence and joy in learning become second nature to you.

The brain booster might not turn you into a genius, but it will definitely help you make the best of your potential, in school and out.

By the same author

Bullies, Bigmouths and So-called Friends

'This brill book is full of tips on how to build up your confidence and look after yourself. We like!'
Bubble

'At last a book that really helps you to deal with the people in your life who are making you miserable.'
The Bookseller

'Unique in teaching children how to boost their self-esteem and so prevent bullying from affecting their lives.' The Independent

'Offers simple strategies for building up confidence so that taunts and teasing have fewer insecurities to feed on.' Sainsbury's Magazine

'There is much in this book that children might find of real help.' Books for Keeps

'An ideal book to be used in schools.'
ChildLine in Schools

'The ideal book for teachers and counsellors ... as well as children themselves.' Education Today

Visit the author's website
www.jennyalexander.co.uk